THE
THIRST
IS REAL

The Guide
to Maximizing
Your True
Potential

GEO DERICE

Copyright 2014 © Geo Derice
All right reserved.

ISBN-10: 061595085X
ISBN-13: 978-0615950853

Please visit www.Geospeaks.com for more information regarding book tour dates, bookings, and speaking engagements of Geo Derice.

DEDICATION

I dedicate this book to God, who blessed me
with the vision to make this book a reality.

I also dedicate this book to my wonderful Mom, Marie Mi-
chele Derice, and my amazing Dad Geoffrion Derice, whose
unconditional love helped me be all that I am
and all I will be.

CONTENTS

Introduction

It was the first day of school. Everything was new. New school, new teacher, new atmosphere and new opportunities awaited me as I entered my first year in high school. For the course of almost a decade I went to the same school, from kindergarten all the way to the 8th grade. My world was always the same; I knew where everything was, so I had no fear at all. As the young generation would say, "I ain't scurred." But high school was completely new for me.

Nothing could have prepared me however for what I experienced during my first class, when the teacher said, "Take out a blank sheet of paper and a pen." Now I was a good student from K-8 so I was prepared with a pen and paper, but what could this teacher possibly have us doing on the first day, when she didn't even know our names yet? The words that followed from her mouth made me feel like I was living a nightmare: "We are having a pop quiz."

Have you ever had a pop quiz before? How do you feel about them? Would you say they are your best friends or would you call them your kryptonite? In my head I felt like saying, "The nerve of this teacher, I don't want to be in high school anymore."

All of the sudden, entering high school was not as enjoyable as I thought it would be. This pop quiz really threw me for a loop, and do you want to know why? Because I did not *expect* it. I was not prepared for the quiz, and so I felt like failure was inevitable. Ever felt that feeling before—a lose-lose situation—a situation where you're darned if you do, darned if you don't?

You're probably wondering what my score was on the quiz, right? Well, I failed, but luckily the teacher was just putting us on notice. She wanted to make the point that in order to succeed in her classroom we would need to be prepared for anything and everything. My thoughts at the time were: *"Boy, does she have a way of getting her point across."* Nonetheless, her tactic worked—she got her point across, and 16 years later the memory of it is as fresh in my mind as the morning breeze of a beautiful summer day.

Similar to my experience the first day of high school, sometimes you may feel like life is a pop quiz. Life has some sudden twists and turns that we never see coming, often catching us by surprise. Now, I don't know about you, but there are some surprises in life that I would *gladly* do without. There are moments of embarrassment that I wish I didn't have to go through, moments of failure that I wish could have been avoided. Why? Because those moments of failures and embarrassments are hard to erase. The experiences of your yesterdays, as hard as they are to let go, often find themselves lingering in your todays, and unfortunately into your tomorrows.

Think back to something that has happened to you in the past that you wish you could forget, something that comes back to haunt you more often than you would like. What was that experience like? What taste did it leave in your mouth? Why do you still remember it, to this day, when it happened days, months, or even years ago? The bitter things in life seem to have a way of sticking around longer than we ever hoped, wished, and imagined.

On the bright side, life isn't *just* moments of bitterness and times we wish we could forget. There are moments in life that everyone wishes would last a little longer or perhaps wishes would never end—memorable events such as receiving a gift or an award, being complimented for hard work or for something well-done. We all love those moments, don't we? But why do those moments happen so infrequently, and more importantly, how can we ensure moments like these happen more often?

First we need to realize that life, as much as it is a pop quiz, is also a test. Pop quizzes are small tests that we do not expect, but life does have tests that we do know are coming, and challenges that we can actually prepare for in advance. But it will require us to see things differently. Instead of looking at the tests as challenges, my challenge to you is to look at them as opportunities—opportunities that will enable you to display what you know or don't know—and you'll learn that *not knowing* is not necessarily a bad thing.

A dear friend of mine Cleveland Linder, who serves as a chaplain and is also a pastor, has an axiom that he often shares when he preaches, and it goes like this:

The me I see is the me I'll be.

First off, the you that you see RIGHT NOW in the mirror is the you that you will be. If I see myself as an overweight person, then that's what I will be. Likewise if I see myself as an intelligent student, that is what I'll be.

So I must see the me that God sees.

I personally wish I came up with this myself. But let's break down what that axiom is actually saying:

The me I see is the me I'll be.

First off, the you that you see RIGHT NOW in the mirror is the you that you will be. Basically you are what you see.

So I must see the me that God sees.

You need to see yourself the way God sees you, not as an object but as his loving child. So if you look in the mirror and feel like you're a mistake, you must understand and believe that's not how God sees you. Long before your parents were born God has a plan for your life. He created you on purpose for a purpose (more on that later).

But if I see myself the way that I've always been

Let's take for example a person who was overweight and lost 100 pounds but still sees the same person, the same size of the person they were before the weight loss. All of the work they've put in didn't matter because they never changed the way they saw things.

then I'm looking at the old me

The next two lines goes on to say that if you see yourself the way you've always been, then you're looking at the old me, meaning the "past" version of yourself.

the unprepared me, and that me won't win.

The final line states that the unprepared me is the one that looks behind them, and a person that does cannot win.

The purpose of this book is to help you to look ahead to the journey that awaits you, not the journey that's behind you. What has happened to you, and what you've seen and experienced in your past, does not have to be your future. There's a lot more in store for you than what meets the eye. The only things you should take from the past are the lessons learned. Anything else is just baggage. It reminds me of seeing people traveling with baggage that exceeds the weight limit. They end up costing you more to carry the extra baggage. This is what not letting go of your past will do to you too.

The Thirst Is Real is designed to guide you step-by-step on how to best win the journey you're on right now! This book will guide you, and prepare you for what is to come, and help you see yourself the way God sees you—a treasure so valuable that he sacrificed his own son in order to bridge the gap between who you are and what you have the potential to be.

I won't pretend that I know your situation—it isn't fair to you—it isn't fair for me to make the assumption that I do. However, what I do know is that what you've been through, good or bad, is nothing compared to what you're going to see happen in your futureif you let it.

Speaking of your future, does it scare you when you think about it? I know for me looking at what's to come and not knowing what will happen, scares me.

Like a scary movie you've watched more than once, the sting that accompanies life's surprise tests will lose its bite. Have you ever wondered why you've never seen a real scary movie more than once? The reason is because you know when the scary moments are coming, so you're no longer scared. This book will help prepare you for those scary moments that would normally trip you up, *if* you hadn't read this book.

I'm excited for the journey we are about to take together. Your dreams, your aspirations, your goals, and your future are on the line. I've been on my knees praying; I've asked friends to pray for this moment. *Which moment*, you ask? The moment we are in now, where you have this book in your hands, and the trajectory of your life will be determined.

I challenge you. Forget what you've been told before about what you can and cannot do, that someone who told you that your dreams are ridiculous, insane, and that you're freaking nuts for thinking you can do that. Smile. You are exactly where you are supposed to be. Hold onto that dream; we're about to plant it, water it, and see it grow.

Chapter One:

The Thirst Is Real

Why name the book *The Thirst Is Real*? You're probably asking yourself that question, and it's a legitimate question. One of the toughest challenges I faced while writing this book was figuring out what the title would be. Before going into why I chose this title and what it means, let's talk about how the world is often used in society. Allow me to paint you the picture.

It's about 6 o'clock in the morning and Robert, who is 16 years old, is just waking up. The first thing he does is look at his smartphone (an iPhone of course), jumps on Facebook to see if Jessica (girl he has a crush on) has posted anything new since he last checked her profile. FYI he last checked a few seconds before falling asleep. He then goes on to her Instagram account because he wants to see if she's posted any new pictures of herself or things she like, not to mention he also knows her Pinterest account (why Jessica has one is beyond me, lol).

Robert then goes to the local train station to go to school. He makes sure he arrives at exactly 7:15am, because he knows that's when Jessica normally takes the train. Jessica arrives at 7:16 am; she's one minute late but good ol' Robert is there. Once at school, prior to the opening bell, Robert sits at the cafeteria table where Jessica is chatting with her friends. When they laugh, Robert laughs and when they sigh, guess what Robert does? Yes, you guessed right, he sighs also (the struggle).

Robert repeats the same behavior during lunch, never getting old of his routine. This isn't just Robert on Mondays, it's Robert EVERYDAY.

Now what would you say Robert is, in regards to Jessica? You'd probably say he's thirsty! Someone on the outside looking in would say, "Man, the thirst is real." Is there any doubt that Robert has an interest in Jessica? Nope! We all know what Robert wants; his actions and behaviors tell the entire story. Robert is borderline stalker.

Now I'm not suggesting that guys and girls take this approach when it comes to getting someone's attention. I can imagine Robert standing up in Stalker's Anonymous and saying, "I read *The Thirst Is Real*, Geo told me this was okay." "Umm Robert, I did not."

While Robert's approach may be looked at as *a bit too much*, and perceived to be negative, Robert is onto something. It's my belief that if we would approach our dreams with this same type of obsession, we would have less "walking dead" people in this world today.

What do I mean by "walking dead" people? I'm not talking about the zombies that we see on the TV show that are always busy eating each other—I'm talking about people, preferably young people, who walk around aborting their dreams.

Norman Cousins, who was an author and a world peace advocate, once said: "The greatest tragedy of life is not death; it's what dies within us while we are living."

I've never forgotten this quote. The impact it has on my life now is the same exact luster it had when I first heard it. In fact, it's the very reason why I believe I exist today; it's the reason why this book was born, and it's the very reason why I did everything in my power to make sure you had this in your hand today!

Many people would say the thing they are scared of the most is death. No one likes to die, nor does anyone want to die. If I was playing Family Feud and they were to ask me the #1 answer for "life's greatest tragedy" my first answer would have been death, my second answer would have been death, and if they needed a third one, I would have said death again! Death is scary.

I recently asked a group of students at William H. Maxwell High School what made death so scary, and here are some of their responses:

-      **Death is scary because it's final. There's no coming back from it.**

-   **Death is scary because we never know when it's coming (you can say that again).**

-   **Death is scary because you have so much you want to do and may never see it happen.**

These are all great responses and they are all true. They are reasons I would have given until I came across the quote by Norman Cousins. But on the flip side, when someone dies but their dreams in life came true, all of a sudden the death isn't as sad. Think about the death of a young person. The thing you often hear when you interview the families are about the future, the dreams of the young person and how those things, because of his or her death, will never be realized. Is death a tragedy? Absolutely. Let's never take that for granted or overlook it. But while death is inevitable (as one day we will all have our time to go), your dreams do NOT have to die before you do!

How can you make sure that your dreams don't die while you are living? My answer—your thirst needs to be real. Like Robert who was obsessed with all things Jessica, you too need to be that thirsty to see your dreams come true.

I met a young man by the name of Chris Howard and he said he wanted to become a comedian when he grew up. Now if that is what he wants, the question we have the right to ask is, "What are you doing to make that happen? What's your thirst like? Are you thirsty to become a comedian? Now this question is not something where you have to do much research to find the answer. When it came to Robert, I didn't have to put a 24 hour watch on him to find out that he liked Jessica. You've heard of the saying "Where there is smoke, there is fire", right? Well, all I had to do was find Jessica (smoke) for me to find Robert (fire).

Throughout this entire book you're going to learn about how to avoid life's greatest tragedy. Our mission together is to get you there. This guide will help you identify your thirst, what you should be thirsty for, the things to look out for, the things you ought to avoid if you want to see your thirst become a reality, and so much more.

This is a journey and I must preface this by saying that every great journey begins with a single step. In the same token, a great journey isn't a sprint.

> **"A great journey is much more a marathon than it is a sprint."**

Will there be moments in a marathon that you'll sprint? Absolutely. However, you'll want to be equipped for the journey ahead. The remaining chapters are the tools to guide you through to winning the race. So without further delay, let's start running.

"The greatest tragedy of life is not death, it's

what dies within us while we are living."

- Norman Cousins

Quick Sips

Being obsessed about your dreams is a sure-fire approach to making sure you don't become a "walking dead" person.

"The greatest tragedy of life is not death; it's what dies within us while we are living" – Norman Cousins

Never let your dreams die before you do.

The key to seeing your dreams come true is to stay thirsty.

Every great journey begins with a single small step.

A great journey is more a marathon than it is a sprint.

Chapter Two:

You Are Thirsty

You are thirsty! Yet you're probably thinking to yourself, *No I'm not*. But we all are. By thirsty I mean we all have desires, things we want, stuff that we are passionate about; we are all thirsty for something. From the moment you were born it was clear you were thirsty. Have you ever met a baby who didn't want something? One minute they are crying for food, another minute they are crying for attention, and the next minute it's crying for the sake of crying (okay that part was a joke).

You cannot help but want something, desire something, or be passionate about something. It's how you were designed to be. There's a quote that says, "If you don't stand for something, you'll fall for anything." Pretty powerful quote, right? Let's look at that with a slight twist, shall we? If you don't want something, don't desire anything, and passionate about nothing, you will fall for what others want for you. I believe Tony Gaskins Jr. said it best: "If you don't build your dreams, someone will hire you to help build theirs." You may not be in a position right now to be hired for a job, but it's worth noting that you better have a dream, you better have a burning desire for something, or else you won't get what you really want. You'll only end up helping someone else get what they want.

Now it's not bad to help others get what they want, or to help others build their dreams, however, there is something wrong with you not building your own. When I meet people who say they are thirsty for nothing, I ask this question:

Let that sink in a little bit. Picture a lonely person waiting at a bus stop, with buses constantly passing them by, with a feeling of neglect and dissatisfaction—feeling like they simply don't matter.

This is exactly why young people aren't thirsty about anything—because they feel like they just exist, and were not created for a purpose. Wrong! You cannot help but be thirsty for something because the One who created you put the thirst inside of you LONG before you ever knew it was there. Do you think it's an accident that you love basketball, have an ear for music or annihilate everyone at the science fair? It's no accident!

It's time you start believing today, that you are not an accident waiting to happen, or an accident that already happened. *You were a blessing waiting to happen*—you have to believe this, understand this, and start living this. You are the stone in a slingshot waiting to be launched into your dreams. How far you land is determine by how thirsty you are.

I have a question to propose. Why when I ask young people what they're thirsty for, (and by thirsty I mean what their dreams, goals, and wants) do they respond with the following words: I don't know.

We've acknowledged that even when you were born and could not speak a word, you had something you were thirsty for. So where did the disconnection take place? Maybe it was when someone told you that what you're thirsty for was a dumb idea. Do you remember ever telling someone an idea only to have them shoot it down? There are many times I've shared some personal dreams or visions for what I see happening with my life and it always hurts when the person you tell it to responds negatively.

I believe this has happened to you. You've been told what cannot happen. You've been told that you are a mistake. Now, the sad thing is some stranger didn't tell you this. I mean if someone walking down the street came up to me and said, "You're stupid," I'd probably karate chop the person. I'm only kidding. But on a serious note, I wouldn't really care. Why? Because the person does not know me. However, to have my mom or dad call me stupid, or tell me what I'm dreaming about is retarded, you know that would hurt! It is my fair assumption that someone you know and care about has shot you down.

You're left with the feeling of not wanting to dream anymore. You don't care about what the future holds because as far as you're concerned, it cannot happen.

11

It's this very reason why we have a bunch of "walking dead" young people on this earth today. You may be 13, you may be 18, but if you have nothing that you're thirsty for, you're really not living. Do not allow yourself to be buried alive.

Let me repeat: You are thirsty for something, or at least you were at some point. If you're going to experience joy, satisfaction, fulfillment, happiness, and a sense of completion, you'll need to revive those dreams once again. You may believe they are impossible today, but allow me to tell you that all things are possible when you believe. The word impossible itself says "I'm Possible".

It was during English Language Arts (ELA) in 3rd grade that my teacher, Mr. Bookbinder, (don't laugh) called me up to do a reading. I remember this day like it was this morning! As I read the word "the", laughs started to break out in the classroom. I cannot remember another time when I was the laughing stock of a room, but I remember from that experience that it's one of the loneliest feelings in the world.

They laughed because of my Haitian accent and how I spoke. They were probably thinking "Man, this kid can't speak"! If you were to ask those students in that room if one day I'd be speaking to hundreds and thousands of kids publicly, they would have said it's impossible. The way my dreams are set up, the way I spell impossible is I'm Possible. Today I'm living my dreams and it's because no matter what happened to me, I knew I was thirsty for something.

Did you know that your body is made up of 50-70% water? You're not only made up of water; you cannot live more than three days without it!

**Just as water makes up 50-70% of your body,
I believe your dreams make up 50-70% of
your life.**

It's no wonder why life simply cannot work without them!

<u>Quick Sips</u>

If you don't want something, don't desire anything, and are passionate about nothing, you will fall for what others want for you and be left dissatisfied.

You cannot help but be thirsty for something because the One who created you put the thirst inside of you long before you knew it was there.

If you're not thirsty for something, then you're not really living.

Nothing is impossible, even the word itself says "I'm Possible".

Your dreams make up 50-70% of your life.

Chapter Three:

What Should You Be Thirsty For?

L L Cool J once had a song called "I Need Love" that was a huge hit in the 80s. At the time, you were not even born yet. I used to listen to this song all the time. The keyword in the title is "need". At the time of listening to this song I didn't really know what I was singing, but love is one of the six human needs we all share. If you're curious as to what you should be thirsty for, we need to start here.

Back in 1943, the idea of the human needs came from Abraham Maslow in his paper titled A Theory of Human Motivation. In it he discussed what motivates humans. I would later on hear from motivational speaker Anthony Robbins who broke down the human needs into six categories. Here they are listed below:

Certainty - the guarantee of you avoiding pain or gaining pleasure.

Uncertainty/Variety - the need for change, the unknown.

Significance - feeling special or important.

Connection/love - deep feeling of closeness with a

person.

<u>Growth</u> - attention on improvement, getting better.

<u>Contribution</u> - helping others or supporting others.

In some regard all the decisions we make stem from the things we need. So when the question beckons what you should be thirsty for, the first place we need to visit is what our needs are. Everything you need falls within the categories listed above. Let's quickly break each one of them down.

Anthony Robbins breaks down the desire/need of certainty to stem back to comfort. We all like to feel comfortable don't we? One funny example is when I get invited to parties that will involve dancing. Now by looking at my picture on the back of this book you wouldn't know this but I was born with two left feet. Dancing is NOT one of gifts I've been blessed with. To avoid being embarrassed I take control of those situations by declining invitations that involve dancing.

When it comes to feeling comfortable we either do as I did in that example and take control, or we relinquish control, placing our faith in someone or something else. No matter which option you choose, being comfortable is where the desire of certainty stems from.

Then there is uncertainty. This is that element of the surprise factor that makes life interesting. Could you imagine if you were watching a television show and the same episode came on all the time? Would you be interested in watching it? Absolutely not! I don't know about you but I would not have an alarm set for 10pm on Thursday if "Scandal" didn't have elements of uncertainty in it. In fact it's the reason why you like scary movies. You like them because of the uncertainty of what is going to happen. It's also the reason why people rarely watch the same scary movie more than once—the element of surprise is all gone.

Next is significance. In the last chapter we talked about not feeling like a mistake or an accident, but instead that you were created on purpose, for a purpose. This is where your significance comes from and our need to have it. We all want to feel special; we all want to feel unique. Would you like it if you were named Michael in a classroom full of Michaels? What about walking down the aisle on your wedding day and every one of your bridesmaids are wearing the same exact dress as you? Wouldn't feel so special then, right? We all want to feel special and important. The good news is that because you were created on purpose, for a purpose, you will find your significance, but you must identify what your thirst is and what makes you unique (more on this in the next chapter).

Like LL Cool J, we all have a deep desire to feel loved. He is not the only one who needs it; you and I both need it, too. It's when we don't feel connected to someone or we don't feel cared about, that we start to act careless! Did you highlight that line? I'll do it for you. It is worth repeating.

> **It's when we don't feel connected to someone**
> **or we don't feel cared about,**
> **that we start to act care-less!**

Every time I prepare a speech for young people, I always remember this quote:

> **"No one cares what you have to say, until they**
> **know how much you care."**

We all want to feel like we are connected to someone, and that someone loves us. I cross my fingers when I say that my hope is that you know you are loved. If you have not been told by someone that you are, please allow me to give you an important revelation that will change your life.

God loves you.

Don't believe me? I'll show you. In the movie *John Q*, Denzel Washington was the father of a child who was in desperate need of a new heart. Long story short, the child was not at the top of the list for a transplant and was facing death. Denzel, feeling desperate, decided to hold a hospital hostage, and when things got really bad he even considered sacrificing his own life so his son could take his own heart. You would say that he loved his son right?

It was a little over 2,000 years ago; God had one son, only one, and he sacrificed him because he wanted YOU! Like Denzel, God showed his love for you through a sacrifice. You are loved! As I write this book I also have come to realize that I love you too. It must be true. I hate to read books, now I find myself writing one. I want to make sure you don't live a life where your dreams aren't realized. You matter. You're important, and let no one tell you differently. The fact you hold this book in your hand is a sign that someone cares enough about you, to make sure you knew the content within it.

The next need is growth. We all have a desire to grow and if we get out of out own way and live freely, it's actually inevitable. Think of yourself when you were a baby: You wanted to walk but could not. As you grew you learned how to crawl, then you learned how walk; it was all steps of improvement and getting better until you mastered it. You have a desire to grow so when you feel stuck in life it's because you aren't growing. Everything in life can be used to help us grow. The good times help us grow in humility and the tough times help us to grow in character. As we grow up we learn to understand more, how to deal with more, and how to do more. There's a quote that says, "The moment you stop learning is the moment you stop living". Why? Because learning is part of the growth process. We need it!

Lastly we have the need of contribution. This focuses on you helping someone else. We all have the need to help one another. The only time this need seems to fade is because we feel like no one is catering to our needs. This is where selfishness begets selfishness and leaves the world looking like a war zone. The national anthem becomes "Me, Myself and I." How do you feel when you give someone else a helping hand? Feels good, doesn't it? There's a story I must share with you.

I was out in Queens on a Sunday afternoon, where my brother's girlfriend was supposed to sing in a choir. I've spoken many times and when I have someone in the crowd supporting me it helps ease my nerves. Knowing how this feels I wanted to do the same for her.

As I was waiting in the line to enter the church, an old lady came up to me and asked if the church was giving out free food. She saw the line and must have thought it was one of those food pantries where they give out food for the needy. I responded to her, "No they aren't giving out free food. This is a line to enter the church for service."

She then walked away disappointed. From the look on her, you knew she was experiencing some hard times. She was short, old, not moving well, and had lipstick all over her teeth. She then came back to me and ask me if I had any money I could give her to get some food to eat.

Let me break out a confession here. Normally I have my dollar bills organized a certain way in my wallet where I know exactly where the $1 bills are and where the $20 bills are. I set it up this way so I don't make the mistake of pulling out the wrong bill in situations just like this. On this day however, when I meant to take out $2 or so, I ended up pulling out a $10 bill. I don't like to take money out and then go back in my pocket to look for other bills, so I gave her the $10. The look on her face after she saw that was priceless and one I won't ever forget. She was so happy that she hugged me. Suddenly the old lady who was struggling to walk down the street, had a little bit more pep in her step. She told me she could actually eat a real meal today and blew me kisses as she walked away.

Never did I feel happier than on that day and it stemmed from me fulfilling my need of contribution. This is nothing special about me; I believe we all have that inside of us. It only gets lost in the mix because we don't think anyone will do something that nice for us. Don't worry about what THEY do; focus on what YOU do. Your reward is in the mail and it's coming.

So back to the question we proposed at the beginning of this chapter:

What should you be thirsty for?

You should be thirsty for opportunities and things that fulfill your human needs. Everything you do needs to fall within those categories. That's where you will find your purpose and your purpose is what gives your life meaning. How do you identify what your thirst is? Turn to the next page :-)

<u>Quick Sips</u>

All the decisions you make stems from things that you need.

We act care-less when there is no one who cares for us or when we feel connected to no one.

To avoid feeling stuck in life be sure you're constantly doing things to grow.

The good times in life help us grow in humility and the tough times help us to grow in character.

When you focus on what you do and ignore the doings of others, you can rest assure your reward is in the mail.

Chapter Four:

How to Identify Your Thirst

It was a regular afternoon. I was cleaning the dining room when I found a notebook with a bunch of scribbles in the back of it. It was on that day I learned of my brother's thirst.

For years Mikey and I religiously played a video game called "Madden". We would play against each other. We would play online as technology advanced, but there was one thing Mikey did which I never caught on to. He would play the 'season' mode in "Madden" where you can act like you own the team, make decisions on which players to keep, which ones to get rid of, which players to draft—the whole nine yards. This part to me was boring; all I wanted to do was beat people. But for Mikey that was all he did. The writings in the back of the notebook were all of Mikey's notes as he worked to create his next championship team.

You're probably saying to yourself, *This kid is obsessed, insane, nuts.* I would say Mikey's thirst was real! He loved to do that stuff and it's no surprise that today he works for the NFL's Indianapolis Colts as a Northeast Area Scout. Little did I know his thirst for evaluating talent and building a winning football team in the video games would lead him to doing the same in real life. Let's go Colts!

How did Mikey find out what his thirst was? It all started with what he loved to do. You couldn't pay me to go ahead and do what he did in that video game, but for him, he did it for free hours upon hours. Why? Because that was his thirst. As he worked on his thirst he was able to fulfill his need for growth (improving his team), significance (making the decisions where he felt important), and elements of uncertainty (not knowing if the team he built was good enough to win). But it all started with something he loved, and that's where YOU identifying what your thirst is begins, too.

There are key questions that you need to ask yourself when it comes to identifying what your thirst is. Before we dive into what those questions are, it's important for you to realize a few things about your thirst and what others will think of it.

When Mikey did those things, I looked at him as someone who was crazy. In fact, I didn't only think it, I told it to him in his face! I couldn't understand why I couldn't play the video games because he was too busy with his pen, writing down information about fake players in a video game. Like Mikey, people will think you are crazy when you find your thirst. It cannot be said with 100% conviction, but those who are "crazy" are often the ones who do things that regular people once thought was impossible. Nelson

Mandela had a quote that said "it's always impossible until it's done". That quote is so true.

There's no better story that shows this more than the story of Roger Bannister. I came across his story while reading a book called *Run to Win* by Christine Caine (I strongly suggest this book). In her book she shares a quote that Roger Bannister said: "The man who can drive himself further once the effort gets painful is the man who will win." Umm, I don't know about you but to push further when something gets painful, that's CRAZY! Well Roger Bannister's thirst was real; his thirst was to be the first man to run a mile in four minutes or less. Running is no easy feat but day after day Bannister pushed his body beyond the limit. The training was painful. Everyday having to train for hours, breaking down his muscles, having to stretch out muscles through soreness, only to do it all over again the next day. Does not sound like something the "average" person would go through, right? Roger Bannister's goal however wasn't to be average, it was to be great! That greatness however, didn't come without a steep price. He knew his thirst and understood there would be pain along the way. But when your thirst is real, as he said, you push further, and eventually you are the one that ends up on top.

What do you love to do? What's the one thing I couldn't get you to stop doing even if I paid you to do so? If you're a singer, I could pay you $100 per day and you wouldn't be able to stop singing. If you love to play basketball, I couldn't pay you to stop playing it, or could I? If I can, then your thirst isn't basketball.

Here are some important questions for you to ask yourself. These questions will help you identify what your thirst is.

1. What are my goals?

2. What do I love to do?

4. What would I do, even if I didn't get paid to do it?

5. If I could do one thing for the rest of my life, what would it be?

6. What do you find yourself lost in (time wise)?

7. Do I have a crazy dream that I have given up on

These questions are just the tip of the iceberg when it comes to identifying your thirst. It's important you do not forget the last chapter when we talked about our needs. Our needs are closely knit to what our thirst is. Following are some other statements that should help you figure out what your thirst is.

1. If I could not fail, I would...

2. If I didn't care what anyone thought of me, I would...

Those two statements are pretty powerful. Take a moment right now to grab a piece of paper and answer the previous questions and the two statements. If you're honest with yourself you will uncover your true passion. You will see some common themes, which will help you to really know what your thirst is.

When you look at the statement of "If I could not fail I would…" think of you being a basketball player and the hoop is the ocean. You wouldn't miss, right? Think the same thought when you answer that statement.

It was recently at a local high school where I was giving a talk that one student asked me, "What made you want to be a motivational speaker?" I get this question a lot and it's a great question actually. I really did not know this was something I wanted to do. The clarity came from a meeting with one of my pastors, Tim Dilena from Brooklyn Tabernacle. I was at a point where I was feeling 'blah'. You know that feeling, don't you? When someone would ask something, my answer would be "it's whatever." If I was paid $1 for each time I heard that word from a young person, I would be rich and never need to work a day in my life.

Pastor Tim is someone I admire. His passion to preach the word of God really caught my attention. It's safe to say I'm a fan of Pastor Tim, but more so a fan of anyone who does something with passion. His thirst is real for preaching the word, and when your thirst is real, no one needs to ask what you love to do; they just see you do it.

27

In our meeting, Pastor Tim asked me, "What's the one thing you would do for the rest of your life, if God came down and said you will never ever have to worry about money again?"

My answer took two seconds to come out. I responded, "Inspire young people to live out their best lives." It was at that moment I realized that nothing makes me happier. There's nothing that gives me a sense of fulfillment like hearing a young person go after their dreams and having me play a small role in it. It's an answer to one of those previous questions: What would you do even if you didn't get paid to do it? For me that would be inspiring people like you and for a while I did speak without being paid.

In fact in February, I decided to take a fast and not use Facebook for the entire month. I don't know if you know anyone obsessed with social media (Facebook or Instagram), but I'm not ashamed to say my thirst is real when it comes to these things. Of course I was no dummy; I picked the shortest month of the year to do my fast ;-)

It was February 2013 that I did this, and I cannot imagine a month in 2013 that I was more miserable than that month. Why was I so miserable? Because every day I try to inspire people through quotes, thoughts, and pictures so they can be filled up with hope for what's to come. Because I was no longer on Facebook I wasn't able to do this like I normally did. It made me sick to my stomach and I couldn't wait for March 1st to arrive. The reward of doing that fast though—it was obvious what my thirst was. The thing you cannot live without—is the thing you thirst for.

<u>Quick Sips</u>

To find out what your thirst is start by asking what is it you love to do.

People we categorize as crazy are often the ones who do things that regular people once thought was impossible.

Your thirst is closely tied to what your needs are.

When your thirst is real no one needs to ask you what it is your love, because it will be obvious and simple for all to see.
The thing you cannot live without is the thing you thirst for.

Chapter Five:

Quench Your Thirst

Dreams don't work unless you do the work to make them happen. Everyone has dreams, but not everyone is willing to work to make them come true. Unfortunately when it comes to seeing successful dreams, people live in the World of Webster. The World of Webster is living life by the dictionary; Only in the dictionary does "success" come before "work".

Your thirst won't work for you unless you WORK for it. Picture your thirst as a seed in the ground; it cannot grow to its full potential without water. Your work is the water that helps your thirst become what it's meant to be. As a football player I always heard my coaches say "You get what you put in", that's where football is a lot like life. If you're to get the most of out of life, you're going to have to give it your all. This is exactly why your thirst has to be real to reach your full potential. Without it, you're simply playing Super Nintendo. Surprisingly, I learned that the game of football is a lot like life.

It was back in 2001 when I had a thirst to be one of the greatest defensive football players to ever play at

Lafayette High School, but the thirst was not going to happen by itself. I had the seed, I knew what I wanted, but how was going to quench my thirst? That would require hard work.

If you were with me back then you would find one of my best friends and I in the gym putting in hours and hours to ensure that we were ready for what was to come. We put in our all and the results were nothing short of spectacular.

The opening game, I registered a team high in tackles, and caught my first interception in my high school career. We went on to win that game against Evander Childs to open the season 1-0. Those results would not have happened if I believed that success would come before work.

It always works the other way around.

Having a strong work ethic is crucial to your success. This includes things like, showing up on time, doing the right thing when no one is watching, being disciplined and giving your all. If you master that alone, you're one step ahead of the game. Laziness is often the stumbling block that gets in the way of achieving your best. Work is an important ingredient to reaching your true potential and maximizing it, but it also requires you knowing what to actually do.

The next step in quenching your thirst is gaining knowledge. I've always heard that knowledge is power, but I believe the correct formula is as follows:

Knowledge (Information/Resources)

+ Application (Work)

= Quench Your Thirst (Power)

When you have the right information or resources and a strong work ethic, and you believe you can do it, you're unstoppable.

Let's consider the famous comedian Kevin Hart. He's a highly successful comedian who can now be seen in television shows, movies—he's pretty much everywhere. One thing his peers could never say was Kevin had no work ethic. They said the exact opposite. They were blown away by how hard he would work.

Unfortunately even with a great work ethic, you won't tap into your full potential without the proper information or resources. It's like trying to push a square peg into a circle hole. It just doesn't fit. When you have the proper information/resources, you add the hard work on top of it and believe you can make it happen, that's when things suddenly change. It's as if the red sea parted ways and you can walk right on through.

In one of Kevin's comedy movies *Laugh at My Pain*, they talked about Kevin receiving the advice to share his personal stories when he was on the stage. That word of advice would change his entire comedic career. Today we laugh at Kevin Hart not only because he is funny, but also because he received the proper knowledge to know how to best connect with audiences. He kept it real.

How do you go ahead and quench your thirst? First you need to make up your mind that you are going to work as hard as it takes to make your thirst become a reality. It's not happening without that mentality. It's planting a seed without pouring any water on it.

Your work symbolizes the water that will help make what you're thirsty(seed) for fully blossom. Once you've made that decision you then get the information to help make it happen. A quick word of advice from Tony Robbins:

Success Leaves Clues

When it comes to learning how to do something, one of the best clues is to find someone who is already doing it. Because they already did it, you can find the shortcuts to getting to the same destination. This is the ONLY reason why I read and why I believe history is important. Reading provides us with wisdom to know what to do. History reveals to us what things worked in the past and what we should avoid.

Speaking of history, back in the summer of 2001 my mom, dad, brother, and I took a trip to Owings Mills, Maryland. That's where I wanted to go for my summer vacation. You're probably asking yourself, "Who wants to go there for a vacation?" I asked my parents to go there so I could see Ray Lewis of the

Baltimore Ravens. They were the defending Super Bowl champions at the time and Ray Lewis was my favorite football player. He was just coming off a Super Bowl MVP and also happened to play the same position I played. If there were anyone I could learn from, it would be him. This was what I did for my summer vacation! While my peers given the same opportunity would pick places like Disney World, Miami, or some Caribbean island, I chose Owings Mills.

My thirst to be the best was real, so I decided to go learn from the best. I did not speak to Ray Lewis, but I paid close attention to everything he did. From the way he interacted with his teammates, to the way he exact stance he stood in, I consumed it all. Those clues I then carried with me my senior year, where I won Defensive Most Valuable Player honors. This all happened because I had the Quench Your Thirst Formula locked in. I believed I could do it; I made up my mind to work hard at it, and lastly, I got the proper knowledge by modeling after someone who was successful at what I wanted to do.

This idea of quenching your thirst cannot be stressed enough. To make sure you got it I want to give you an example of how you can apply this to the thirst you've identified.

It was back in November of 2013 when I spoke to a classroom of six students. Now I was disappointed that only six showed up, but there was one particular young man who really caught my eye. I asked him what he was thirsty for and he said he wanted to own his own restaurant. I responded, "What are you doing to quench your thirst?"

His answered surprised me. He said "I watch television shows about restaurants, TED talks online about running businesses, and study one of the best restaurateurs in the world. This was a 13 years old boy! Do you think this young man will see that thirst realized? I firmly believe he will, it's just a matter of time, especially with a thirst THAT real.

Do yourself a favor and commit the Quench Your Thirst Formula of having Knowledge + Hard Work + Believing in yourself to memory. I firmly believe if you have those three elements in place, we won't be questioning if your thirst is real, it will be obvious.

<u>Quick Sips</u>

Dreams don't work unless you do.

The only place that success comes before work is in the dictionary.

To get the most out of life, you have to give it your all.

Quench Your Thirst Formula: Knowledge + Application + Believe

Your work symbolizes the water that will help make your thirst (the seed) grow.

Chapter Six:

Watch Out For Sodas

"You cannot hang out with negative people and expect to live a positive life." This was a quote by Joel Osteen, who happens to pastor one of the biggest churches in the United States. One thing that holds people back is who they hang out with. It stops them from maximizing their true potential. If our thirst is a deep desire to getting what we want, then consider negative people the very thing that dehydrates you from getting there.

When you're dehydrated you're incapable of functioning at your best. The body is made up of 50-70% water, but when you are dehydrated it's as if your body becomes a desert. Negative people have the potential to dehydrate your true potential. They prevent you from being able to quench your thirst, and they stop you from reaching your best. How so? They distract you from focusing on the goals you have.

One beverage that dehydrates you is soda. Soda is a sugary drink that is filled with empty calories. It is also, a beverage that dehydrates you. It leaves you with a short sugar high, only to suck the 'fake energy' out of you. That's why all negative people and things from this point forward will be called, "sodas".

It's important in your quest to maximizing your true potential that you watch out for the sodas. Sodas are located everywhere and are out to get anyone who is thirsty. Listen to that statement carefully. Sodas are everywhere and they are out to get anyone who is thirsty.

Negative people don't go after negative people, there's no fun in that. What they want more than anything else is to have some positive people come join their parade of misery. Because they aren't happy with their own lives, they adopt the idea of "the more the merrier".

Motivational speaker Craig Valentine once told a story about crabs in a barrel. He talked about how when one crab tries to get out the barrel, the others pull it back in. This is what sodas do to those who are thirsty. The minute you look like you're about to achieve something they come out of nowhere to kill your vibe.

You've heard of the saying "bad company corrupts good morals" right? Well bad company demolishes good dreams too. Be careful with whom you hang around with. All it takes is being at the wrong place, at the wrong time, with the wrong people to see your entire life change.

My senior year I was a part of a program called Spark. The program was designed to educate students on life issues like sex, drugs, and violence. You don't know this about me but I was a 90 average student, never did drugs, and the only violence I knew was on the football field when I tackled someone. So why would I be a part of a program like Spark? It's real simple. The free trips!

There was one trip that honestly changed my entire life and it really reminded me that it's important to watch out for sodas. The trip was to a prison out in Staten Island. There we sat in a room with a bunch of prisoners who were convicted of many different crimes. There were some of them who were there for 15 years and others who had life sentences. But, what changed my life was the stories I heard of how they got there.

One man talked about how he got into jail at the age of 18 years old and he was doing a life sentence. I do not remember his name but let's say it was Anthony. Here's Anthony's story as I remember it:

One day I was hanging out in my neighborhood when I saw a group of friends from around the way. The group of friends was up to no good. They were about to beat up an enemy of the group. As we approach this person my group of friends started to beat up on the guy. The man ended up in a coma and all my friends including myself were arrested on assault charges. It's worth noting I didn't participate in the fight at all. I was simply at the wrong place at the wrong time. A few days later, after none of us admitted to who did the fighting, the man in the coma died. All of the sudden what started out as an assault charge was upgraded to a murder charge. Once again no one stood up to say who did the fighting, and because I was hanging in the wrong crowd, I suffered the same punishment they did. My crime that day was not beating a man to his death; my crime was hanging out with the wrong crowd.

As you can imagine this story broke my heart. 15 years from that incident I stood there watching a man, who was my age when he went to jail, all for a crime he did not commit. Now we might say that it was wrong for him to go to jail because he did not do anything, but sometimes all it takes hanging out with the wrong crowd. He hung out with sodas that day and they dehydrated him costing him his freedom.

When you face someone or something that takes you away from what you're thirsty for, those are sodas that need to be kept at a distance. You cannot have them because they work against you, not for you.

Then there is also the other kind of sodas, haters. You know who I'm talking about—the people who see you're about something and decide they've got nothing better to do than to tell you what you cannot do. What you have to realize about haters is they don't hate you. They actually hate themselves. Why? Because you're a reflection of what they wish to be.

Your focus should be your living water, your dreams. What you identified as your thirst in Chapter Four is what needs to be your driving force. Without keeping your eyes on the prize, you will end up in the wrong place.

Too many times the reason we don't reach our destination has nothing to do with a lack of desire. It's a lack of a focus that becomes our kryptonite. Sodas suck your energy and take away your focus. Instead of you focusing on your thirst they have you focusing on things that aren't important. They often place fear in you. They tell you something is impossible and you start to believe that they're right. However, my mentor Paul Reddick and my close friend Cleveland John Linder, once told me what fear stands for and I want to share it with you today.

F - False

E - Evidence

A - Appearing

R - Real

This means that what sodas are telling you doesn't even exist! It looks like evidence, it appears real, but the evidence is a lie. When they tell you that what you're thirsty for is ridiculous, they are trying to make you full of fear. And often times because they have lost the courage to pursue their dreams, they end up trying to get you to give up on yours. Don't let that happen to you.

When you watch out for sodas, you can ensure that

you're in a state of mind where success is inevitable. They won't suck away your knowledge, they won't take away your work ethic and they won't take your faith away. Watch out for them and remember the Quench Your Thirst Formula. Those are important keys to unlocking your maximum potential.

<u>Quick Sips</u>

You cannot hang out with negative people and expect to live a positive life.

Negative people dehydrate your true potential.

Sodas are everywhere and their job is to suck the potential out of anyone who is thirsty for something.

Bad company demolishes good dreams.

Failure to reach your goals is due to a lack of focus.

F.E.A.R - False Evidence Appearing Real

Quenching Your Thirst Formula is your key to unlocking your maximum potential.

Chapter Seven:

How to Stay Hydrated

"Even a broken clock is right twice a day." When I first heard this quote I could not help but laugh. The things that are most funny are often true, and that quote is so true. But what is the quote about? The point of the quote is it's not enough to be right sometimes. It's much better to be right all the time. Now what does this have to do with your thirst and the idea of staying hydrated?

Ray Lewis said it best: "Greatness are small things done well day after day." The first part is awesome in itself; greatness is not all the big stuff we see, it's more of the little things we do not see.

The real important part of the quote is the end of it, where it says "day after day". What you do everyday becomes a habit. If someone told you they loved you only once in your lifetime, would you even believe it? Chances are no. However, if you were told that every single day you'd be more likely to believe it right? When it comes to your thirst being real, you must stay hydrated. You must not be just right twice a day like a broken clock. You need to be a working clock that is right for all 86,400 seconds of the day.

Last chapter we talked about negative people and how they dehydrate you, but what do you do to stay hydrated? For starters hang around others who are about something. In other words, "Their thirst is real." There is nothing like hanging around a bunch of go-getters. Famous motivational speaker Jim Rohn once said, "You are the average of the five people you spend the most time with." Just like hanging around negative people sucks the life out of you, taking away your ability to fulfill your true potential, hanging around positive people has poured life into you, feeding your potential to succeed.

Selecting whom you hang around with is probably one of the most important decisions you will make in your life. I repeat, selecting whom you hang around with is probably one of THE most important decisions you will make in your life. To stay hydrated you need to be around those who are thirsty for something. There's no group of people more destructive than those who are thirsty for nothing at all. The only thing more dangerous is a bunch of them hanging around each other. Now that's a nightmare.

Hanging around positive people is only one piece of staying hydrated. Another thing is—don't be a know-it-all. Don't act like you don't know someone who thinks they know everything. That person might be you. I did not know this about me, but my close friends, pointed out that I'm as stubborn as a mule. In other words, I act like I know it all. When you act like that you're basically a rock, when you should be a sponge. As a rock, you cannot absorb new information or new knowledge because nothing can go inside of you. As a sponge however you soak up all the information.

Many elders come to me and tell me the issue with young people is they don't care what grown folks have to say, they think they know it all. The minute you stop learning is the day you stop living. Don't be a rock, be a sponge. Remember the formula to quenching your thirst? Knowledge + hard work + believe/faith. If you're a rock, then you are missing the knowledge element of the formula and will fail to quench your thirst adequately.

Another element to staying hydrated is never being satisfied. Complacency is the word that many people use when it comes to being satisfied. It's that feeling you get when you feel like you've made it. When you feel like you've made it, that's when you actually get left behind. The same enthusiasm you started off with, that's the one you need to have day in and day out. That energy, that burning desire, that thirst needs to be real! Please remember this fact because the pain that is caused by complacency is something you'll never want to experience. I unfortunately did.

It was about four to five years ago that I started working for a man by the name of Ryan Lee. He was a mentor of mine when I was a personal trainer. I didn't know much about marketing myself but I knew I wanted to succeed at it. Ryan was the marketing guru personal trainers went to for advice. Because I was not good at selling personal training I had little money to go attend Ryan's marketing boot camp.

His boot camp was a 3-day seminar, teaching you everything you need to know about marketing as a personal trainer and how to build a business. This was where I could get the knowledge I needed become a financially successful personal trainer. Not having the money to attend, I practically begged one of Ryan's colleagues to volunteer at the boot camp in exchange for a free ticket. News flash, nothing in this world is free. I didn't pay for the event, but I was put to work.

Months later I saw Ryan online using Yahoo Messenger, now this is the equivalent of you being a music artist and finding Jay-Z online. You know he probably won't respond if you write to him, but I had nothing to lose so I wrote Ryan anyway. He was in the middle of promoting his book *The Millionaire Workout*. He offered to coach me for one hour, if I could sell five copies of his book. I had no idea how I was going to do this, but if you were there, you would have seen me looking online high and low to see how I could make this happen.

Four sales later, Ryan reached out to me and said, "Wow Geo, you were able to sell four of my books today; how did you do that?"

I created a YouTube video after seeing some strategy

online on how to get more views on your YouTube videos. My thirst was real; I wanted that coaching for one hour with Ryan. Little did I know that action would lead to Ryan offering me a full time job. He never asked for a job resume, he never asked what college I went to, but because he saw how THIRSTY I was, he offered me a job. I'm not suggesting you don't go to college. What I am saying however, is when your thirst is real, and you work towards it, nothing can stand in your way. Success will come find you.

I share this story because it's where the pain comes in. After working with Ryan for years and doing a great job, (I was the Vice President of the company), I began to take my foot off the gas. I started relaxing more; that go-getter attitude, my thirst that I had in the beginning started to fade away. I thought I made it; I grew satisfied, and because of this my performance dropped. I was still doing my work, but it was not at the capacity I once did it.

Then on a regular September morning, I received a call from Ryan. Rarely did Ryan call me in the morning. But oblivious to what was about to happen, I picked up with a smile on my face. At the end of the conversation, my smile was replaced by a frown with a side of tears, when Ryan relieved me of my duties (nice way to say fired). As you can imagine I was completely devastated. Here I had a job where I didn't have to leave home; I was making good money, and all of the sudden I was unemployed.

Can you guess the main reason why I was released? I didn't stay hydrated. I let my thirst dry out. It was as if my thirst became a desert where no water could be found.

<u>Quick Sips</u>

Greatness is small things done well day after day.

You are the average of the five people you spend the most time with.

One of the most important decisions you'll ever make is whom you hang out with.

The minute you stop learning is the day you stop living.

When you feel like you've arrived that's when you get left behind.

Chapter Eight:

Desert Storm

The road to success is not straight. I never really knew what this meant until I read a poem about it, and realized the comparisons. Here's the poem below:

<u>"The Road to Success is Not Straight"</u>
There is a curve called failure,
A loop called confusion,
Speed bumps called friends,
Caution lights called family,
You will have flats called jobs.
If you have a spare called determination,
An engine called perseverance,
Insurance called faith,
A drive called God,
You will make it to a place called success!

This poem depicts exactly what the journey of success looks like. Many times we think that the road is easy, but in reality it's not. Anything worth having comes at a price and sometimes that price is steeper than we think. What happens next when you fail is what will determine if you succeed or not.

When I was fired from my job after not staying

hydrated, it capped off the darkest year of my life. It was earlier that year my girlfriend of 6 years and I broke up for good, too. So as you can imagine having that happen in January and then September to lose your dream job, I felt like a total loser! I found myself in desert storm.

Desert storm is when you find yourself in a situation when things just seem to be falling apart and you don't know what to do. Life is going to have obstacles, and it will involve situations that you're not going to like.

The reason we go nuts when things go wrong is because we never see it coming. It's like those uncertain moments in a scary movie that get our heart. We panic, lose sight of the bigger picture, and feel like our life is over.

Another part of desert storm is loneliness. Desert storm isn't a place where someone wants to be with you. There's nothing there! Have you ever felt like no one understood what you were going through? It's like Will Smith during the movie *I Am Legend*. He was all alone, just him and his dog.

It's a desert, there's no water; it's hot and muggy, and the conditions are extremely uncomfortable. If you are facing tough times, tough challenges right now and feel all alone, you're in desert storm. Let me offer you some advice. **Do not make a permanent decision in a temporary situation**. I bold that statement because many people have taken their life away because of their temporary situations. I know that desert storm is lonely, and it feels like there are no answers. It's in those moments you have to remember that God loves you, and he will never leave your side. Even when he appears far, he's closer than you think. Life is not a straight line. You're going to face moments that are awesome and other moments where they suck. But just like it never rains forever, the bad times will stop, and the sun will shine again. You just have to believe!

The journey towards what you're thirsty for up prior to this chapter may have seemed easy. All I've got to do is accept the fact I'm thirsty, identify what I'm thirsty for, watch out for sodas, and stay hydrated—simple enough. That is true for someone who is starting off with a clean slate, but I believe very few of us start off that way.

We all have baggage; we've all got things in our past that have entered into our present. As a result we hold our future hostage. In order to catch your future, you must let go of your past.

In 1999 my assistant football coach came to me and told me my head coach thought I was a waste of talent on the varsity football team. I did not have any supporters cheering me on at those times. I was alone. I was in desert storm. It was dark, it was lonely, and the hope that I had was little to none. But what do you do when you feel this way? How do you press on, when things just appear to be all against you?

This reminds me of Michael Jordan's story when he tried out for the varsity basketball team. He was told he was not good enough and didn't make the team. Can you imagine what that felt like? Rejection sucks. I hate it, and I'm pretty sure you hate it too. There's nothing like hearing the word "no" when you desperately want to hear the word "yes". When Michael Jordan was told no, he found himself in desert storm.

Tyler Perry who is known for his amazing plays and the character Madea knows too well about desert storm. Tyler Perry was homeless, abused as a child, told by Hollywood that his screenplays would never make it onto the big screen; he also, found himself in desert storm.

Thomas Edison failed 10,000 times when he tried to discover the light bulb! I don't know about you, but failing once is hard enough to bounce back from. People on the outside probably looked at him like a hopeless man who just didn't have a clue. Edison was in desert storm.

As you can see many people have found themselves in desert storm at some point or another. They have failed many times, they have been told what they could not do, and many of them were told no. As the poem in the beginning of the chapter says, the road to success is not straight. The road often leads you down a road called 'desert storm'. What you do there will determine if you will get out alive. Let me show you how

<u>Quick Sips</u>

The road to success is not straight.

Anything worth having comes at a price.

In order to catch your future, you must let go of your past.

What you do during desert storm will determine how soon you get out.

Chapter Nine:

Finding Your Oasis in Dry Places

Between a rock and a hard place, that's where I found myself when I was let go from my job. I felt hopeless. I was depressed, discouraged, and became a human couch potato. If you were with me, you would have had to poke me to see if I was even alive. At that point I was like a desert, dry with no sign of life.

Have you ever been in a situation like that—a place where unfortunately things just didn't go as you planned? This is a feeling that we all go through. Even super highly motivated, successful people go through bouts like these in their lives. However, knowing this does not make things any easier.

If we know those dry moments are going to happen then what can we do about them? For starters let me say that as much as we'd like to avoid these dry places, they are inevitable. The frustration comes from us not realizing that just because our thirst is real, that the struggle isn't real too. Anything worth having does not come easy. If it were so easy, everyone would be great, but that's not how it works. Greatness requires work.

Let's take for example a diamond, which we know are women's best friends. There's a saying that goes, "No pressure, no diamonds." In fact, in order for diamonds to form, a tremendous amount of heat and pressure is necessary. The pressure is like having thousands of men stomping on your foot. When it comes to temperature we are talking about 2,000 degrees Fahrenheit. Without pressure diamonds cannot form and without some dry places, you won't be able to build the character needed to support the greatness you were destined for.

The key to making it through these dry places is finding your oasis, a place of peace, safety or happiness in the midst of trouble or difficulty. There is no oasis without there being dry places. That means an oasis can only be found during times of difficulty. How do you find it? One way is taking control of your mind.

Let me not overlook the things you're going through because that's the last thing I want to do. There's a good chance you've been through things that I cannot even imagine. Some of those things I'd imagine would take the average person down for the count. I believe however, that you reading this book is not an accident. You are still here because the potential inside of you is a lot bigger than the circumstances that are trying to dry you up. The oasis, the place of happiness, is something you can attain, but you have to believe that. It also does not happen automatically.

For you to find your oasis in dry places you have to

realize that you need a positive mindset. I remember hearing the statement, "No pain lasts forever" when Ray Lewis talked about some of his dark days battling injuries and other life situations. Let's break down that quote. The quote isn't saying that there is no pain. In fact it acknowledges that pain exists. What it says however is that it won't last forever. Too many times we give up because we think we'll be in the dry place forever. We wish that the pain would just go away. Let me tell you something, it will go away.

You just have to hold on!

A big part of you having a positive mindset is your self-talk. We think that people who speak to themselves are crazy, but if that were so, we would all be considered crazy. I'm not talking about the person who walks in the street and talks out loud to himself or herself; I'm talking about the inner voice inside of you that only you can hear. Those moments where in the dry places we say to ourselves things like, "I don't matter", "I give up", and "This is impossible." We've all been there. That's where I found myself after losing my job. I was worthless, and I knew this because it's all I told myself.

My mentor Paul one day texted me and told me that I had to snap out of this funk. Honestly, his words that day went through one ear and out the other because my depression wouldn't allow me to hear him or anyone else. That's what depression does to us; it makes us like a hard rock. Try this experiment. Go find a rock and talk to it. Tell it to move and see what happens.

It won't budge and it doesn't matter what you say to it or the motivation you provide the rock, it simply won't move. Thank God however you're not a rock. You're a human being that has emotions, feelings, and life inside of you. The problem comes when our hearts become like a rock.

Speaking with Paul was good though; because when I had negative self-talk he hydrated me by speaking positivity into my life. He would tell me that I had potential. He would tell me that it was just a season I was going through to prepare me for better things. How awesome was that? You mean to tell me that this was a season and not the way my entire life was going to be? I'm telling you the same thing today. The dry place you're in now is just a season. We have winter, spring, summer and fall, and no matter what, these seasons change, and so will yours. This place you're in right now is temporary, so I'd hate for you to go ahead and make a permanent decision while you're in a temporary situation.

Whatever you say you are, you will be. So start to speak positive things into your life. One quick way to do this is to never end a negative comment with a period, use a comma. This is one way I govern my self-talk to make sure I don't take ownership over any negativity. The best way to show you how this is done is through an example.

Example 1: I'm so fat. (Negative)

Example 2: I'm so fat, but I'm not going to be for very much longer!

Instead of ending a negative statement with a period, always use a comma and finish your statement saying something positive.

The power of death and life is found in the tongue according to the Bible. I don't know if you can remember, but back in the day we had a show called *Family Matters*. It had a character name Steve Urkel who had many famous sayings such as, "Did I do that" and "I know you are but what am I". One of his favorites was, "Stick and bones may break my bones, but your words won't ever hurt me." How many of you know that is a complete lie?

Words do hurt and sometimes they can create a hurt inside of us that we cannot shake easily. It's why we must speak positive words to ourselves, because there are a lot of sodas in this world that will tell you the negative stuff.

So we have positive self-talk as one way to find your oasis in dry places. Another way is helping someone while they are in their dry place. Let me warn you—this is not easy. One thing that people who are miserable like that do is throw these famous parties. You know what kind of parties I'm talking about, right? Pity parties! Misery loves company; it's like the crabs in a barrel story. The crabs at the bottom feel stuck and miserable thus when one has the courage to leave, the rest of them pull that one back in.

One morning I received a text from one of my friends and mentor Monte Sanders. He was also my personal trainer. I was in a dry place in my life and Monte was one of the few people I trust who could hydrate me, sharing some words of wisdom. I told Monte I didn't know how to get out of the funk I was in and he shared the following: "When you take care of someone else's troubles, God will take care of yours."

I didn't really get it at first to be honest with you. When we are feeling upset and in trouble the last thing we want to do is think about someone else's trouble. Can I get a "word up" on that one? It's unconventional to think of someone else's pain when you've got your own. But sometimes the way to breaking your pity party is to crash someone else's pity party and help them out of it.

When the advice Monte shared finally started to settle in, that's when Paul crashed my pity party. As I helped others with their tough situations, it took attention away from my problems. Sometimes just that little relief, of not focusing on where you are, is the break you need to feel good again.

Helping my friends and hydrating them with whatever I had available, helped me to fulfill my need of contribution as we talked about in Chapter Three. I felt significant again, because someone thanked me for my help.

When you are trying to reach your full potential, dry places will come, but when you remember to stay positive, watch your self-talk, and hydrate others when they are in their dry places, you will find your oasis.

<u>Quick Sips</u>

Without pressure, there are no diamonds.

The potential inside of you is bigger than the circumstances around you.

No pain lasts forever.

Do not make a permanent decision in a temporary situation.

Never end a negative comment with a period, always finish it with something positive.

When you take care of someone else's troubles, God will take care of yours.

Chapter Ten:

Being a Water Fountain

"In helping others, we shall help ourselves, for whatever good we give out completes the circle and comes back us". This was an important quote said by Flora Edwards. When you're in a desert, when things appear to look dark, the tendency is to do nothing at all. Instead of counting your blessings, you begin to count your problems. That's a recipe for a disaster waiting to happen.

We've heard many times that good things come to those who wait, well that's not true in my opinion. For those who wait, you end up with the leftovers of those who didn't.

The best part of thanksgiving is the fact you don't have to cook for a few days. What's funny is the leftovers taste better than when you first had the meal. However, those are the only times that leftovers are good. You don't want to live a life where you end up with the leftovers of others. That's what you end up with when you sit around doing nothing.

While in desert storm it's important that you become a water fountain. When my throat is dry and I'm in a public place, I desperately look for something to drink. My savior is found when I stumble upon a water fountain. It helps get rid of the dryness that I had in my mouth. Likewise when you are in a dry place, sometimes your words of encouragement to someone else can be the only water they'll ever find. And as Flora Edwards said, it's in helping others that the circle comes around full, back to us.

One of the greatest ways to becoming a water fountain is volunteering. Volunteering is something that I've had the pleasure of doing many times and it never gets old. The ability to go ahead and help someone in need is amazing. It helps my need for contribution, my need of significance and by sharing love with someone else they share it back with me. This cannot be underestimated.

Do you ever wonder why when celebrities get in trouble or when someone gets in trouble they often get a sentence of community service? I don't have the facts to tell you why, but I sure can guess. I believe they are given community service because number one—it gives them something productive to do. I've heard many times, idle time is the devil's playground. This basically means that when you are 'bored' or have 'nothing to do', that's when evil things begin to creep into your mind. A lot of young people when asked why did you commit this crime respond "I was bored". So when you commit a crime, rather than putting you in jail where you will do nothing, they give you community service, keeping you occupied.

Community service also gives you a sense of contribution and significance as we alluded to earlier. We often do some pretty ridiculous things because we want attention.

I don't know about you but things like twerking, or slap cam that I see a lot on the Internet, is all an attempt to get attention. Don't get me wrong, wanting attention is not a bad thing. We all have a desire to receive attention; that makes us human. If you're a cat then yes you don't mind being ignored, but I think we are more like dogs. We want love and affection. We want to receive attention from others. The advantage of community service over activities such as twerking or playing games like slap cam with your friends, is there are only positive consequences.

Activities such as twerking, performing violent acts just to show you're tough or not afraid, do have negative consequences. For the twerk-lovers out there, you devalue yourself when you're just shaking your butt to the camera. I'm sure there is so much more to you then a butt shaking up, down and all around. You have a heart, a brain, and a beautiful spirit inside of you; let those be the things that shine. The last thing you want to be significant for is being the person that shakes their butt on camera for a few likes from people who don't even care about you. Let your personality, your passion, and the things you love be what represents who you are.

Twerking is mostly for women, but when it comes

to guys, we want to show that we are macho and tough. It's why the games such as "knockout" have gained so much popularity. Ask yourself this question: If I have to punch someone for no reason to get praise from my friends, are they really my friends? When you punch someone just for the sake of it, it's actually an assault. It's a crime you're committing.

Now I know many people do it and get away with it, so they think *if I wasn't caught doing it, then it's as if it never happened.* I think we know better than that! The person who is on the receiving end of those acts is someone's brother, father, mother, aunt, or sister. The very game you find funny isn't something you'd laugh at if someone you cared about were the victim of it, right?

Being a water fountain is you hydrating others. When you hydrate others you begin to put the boomerang effect into motion. When you throw a boomerang, it comes right back to you. So like a boomerang, when you help hydrate other, helping them fulfill their thirst, it comes back to you, helping you to fulfill your thirst as well.

This reminds me of an epic moment in my life I have to share with you.

There's a friend of mine named Justin Reid, who is a photographer. He takes photos during the young adult church service I attend at Brooklyn Tabernacle called Transitions. After seeing him take so many pictures I decided to hire him to take some photos of me. Justin took the photo of me on the back cover of this book. Now I could have easily hired someone else to take pictures and it possibly could have been cheaper, so why didn't I? I honestly wanted to support Justin because he has a thirst for photography and his dream is to become a full-time photographer. That's his thirst, that's his passion. It's what he loves to do.

One afternoon I went up to Manhattan to take photos during Justin's lunch break from his day job. While others go eat during their lunch break, Justin was quenching his thirst. The scene was Central Park, a place I've been to only twice in my 29 years of living in New York City. Justin did a great job with me and I could tell he was doing something he really loved. At that moment Justin's photography and my hiring him to do what he loves, made me his water fountain.

A few months later while attending a wedding I met a wonderful lady named Genice Reid. This was Justin's mother. Justin told his mom that I was a motivational speaker and she seemed intrigued to know more about it when we met. After we spoke, she mentioned that perhaps someday I can go speak to a group of students she's involved with at a local high school. I responded, "Sure," but wasn't sure if it would ever happen. Time did go on and I never heard from Mrs. Reid again.

At this point is where we normally would give up and say that it was not meant to be. I'd be lying to you if I said those thoughts did not creep into my mind.

However, at a marriage conference at the church, Mrs. Reid and I crossed paths once again. She mentioned that I should come speak to the students and this time, she had a date.

December 19th, 2013 was the date that changed my life. I had a speaking engagement set up by Mrs. Reid at Maxwell H.S. in East New York. The speech was a huge success and the feedback from the young people there really encouraged me to go ahead and make this book a reality. Little do they know that they were my water, they hydrated me to help fulfill what I was thirsty for, inspiring young people to tap into their full potential.

I'm forever grateful for the time spent with the HOSA group at Maxwell H.S. and further more grateful for Mrs. Reid, Ms. Cummings, Ms. Scott, the assistant principal, and principal for the opportunity to share with the young people there.

The reason I shared this long story with you is for you to see what being a water fountain looks like and what it ultimately does. Being a water fountain to Justin made it all come around full circle back to me. I had no idea that was going to happen when I did it, nor did I do it for that reason.

When you focus on just being a water fountain, you will help those who are thirsty, and in return your thirst will be filled too! Do not underestimate the value of helping others. Remember that great things don't happen to those who do NOTHING, it happens to those who DO SOMETHING.

Quick Sips

It's in helping others that the circle comes around full, back to us.

Let your personality, your passion, the things you love be what represents who you are.

When you help hydrate others, others will help hydrate you.

Great things come to those who DO.

Chapter Eleven:

The Construction of the Well

Imagine walking into a movie theatre, not knowing what movie they were going to show. How would you feel? You would probably be filled with curiosity, filled with questions such as: what is the title of the movie, what is it about, what genre is it—the list goes on and on. What about if the movie was of you? Pause for a second. When you read that what was your first thought? If it were I, my first thought would be panic!

Say the world was going to watch a movie of your life; would you be comfortable with them seeing it? I wouldn't. There are parts of my life that I'm not too proud to show others. Can we agree that you too, have parts of your life you'd rather no one know about?

When it comes to someone watching your life on video, we should get to the point where we aren't worried about what they see. But, that's only possible when our thirst is real and we've constructed a well that is built off our thirst. Live a life with such passion that those who see you will be thirsty to do the same.

Which would you rather have: bottles of water, or a well? A well, right? The well means you have a constant source of water. In third world countries a little bit of water is not going to do the trick to save the people. However, build a well and suddenly we've developed a sustainable solution that can serve them for life. This is why you need to focus on constructing your well! It's not enough that you just get hydrated every now and then, or to be thirsty just for a short period of time. You want to be thirsty and have that become your lifestyle!

This book was about you and the journey towards reaching your full potential, nothing more—nothing less. The goal is for you to become successful in all that you do. This means success in the classroom, success in your friendships, success reaching your dreams, success in fulfilling the six human needs—it's all about successfully maximizing your full potential in all areas of life.

Take a look at some of the top people in any industry and you'll see how they've constructed a well for themselves and today are able to find success in all areas of their lives. For example we can talk about popular rapper, Jay-Z. Many know him as one of the greatest rappers of all-time. His thirst was real from the get go when it comes to dominating the music industry. He went from rapping to owning his own record label, but he didn't stop there. He stayed thirsty and went on to create his own clothing line, which has made him millions. Recently he's released his very own cologne. Chances are success will come with that too. Jay-Z built himself a well, and he lives out a lifestyle of being thirsty.

Hopefully you've acknowledged by now that it's important for you to be thirsty for something instead of nothing, and how to go ahead and make the most out of your thirst. The recipe to success is different for different folks. I'd be a fool to tell you that there's only one-way to becoming successful. However, like Martha Stewart said, "There is a single ingredient that all success recipes have and that's PASSION."

I'm an avid Apple lover. By apple I'm not talking about the fruit, although an apple a day keeps the doctor away. When I say Apple, I mean the company that created the iPhone, iMac and the iPad. I've had them all; and still use them all today. They say that those who love Apple are a bunch of people who buy them because of what Apple represents.

Apple is a company that was built off the shoulders of Steve Jobs. Steve Jobs is one of my role models. Honestly there is no one who personifies the theme "the thirst is real" like he did. The man wore the same clothes every single day.

I know you're thinking, he must have smelled. No. He wore the same clothes as in the same color, same type of clothes. Steve Jobs always had a black turtleneck on, with some jeans and that's it. He was so focused on building Apple he didn't have time to waste focusing on what clothes to wear.

Talk about being thirsty. He was!

Steve Jobs had a popular quote that went like this: **"You have to have a lot of passion for what you are doing because it is so hard if you don't; any rational person would give up."**

He didn't say you need a little passion—he said you need a lot of it! That's the reason you need to construct yourself a well and build a lifestyle where others can see that "your thirst is real."

A little bit of water won't cut it when you walking around in your desert storm, but when you build yourself a well, there's nothing that you cannot overcome. You will become unstoppable. You'll be well on your way to maximizing your full potential, you will have a constant source of water, so when the sodas show up you'll be well hydrated.

Quick Sips

The single ingredient all recipes of success have is passion.

Without passion when things get hard, you'll want to give up.

Always stay thirsty so your desire for greatness doesn't dry out.

Epilogue

Passion will make you do a lot of things you never thought you could do or would want to do, but when you do it, you're left wondering how you did without it. Today I attempt to live every facet of my life with passion. In areas where I'm not as passionate, I use it as a sign that it's probably something I should not do.

You're a person who has dreams, hopes, and deep burning desires, just like I do. How we go about getting them however is different. The common thing is we will all need to have passion to get there—passion to pass the obstacles, and passion to go on whether people are cheering or hating on you.

Your past may have been less than ideal, and I am sorry for what has happened, but I'll be really sorry if what happened in the past stops you from what is going to happen in your future.

I heard a quote from a football player; he said, "When the past comes calling, send it to voicemail because it has nothing new to tell you." For you, my wish is that you are bold enough, courageous enough, and have a thirst so real you can't help but send your past to voicemail.

Like a diamond, all the pressure/pain that has come from your past will catapult you into the bright, shining future you have ahead of you. My attempt to contribute to your future is what you hold today in your hands. I'm forever grateful that you allowed me to go on the beginning of your journey towards maximizing your true potential.

Please do not hesitate to write to me and share with me your stories. There is no greater reward for me than knowing how you're doing and how much closer you are to fulfilling your thirst. I can be reached at geo@geospeaks.com. I look forward to hearing from you.

Acknowledgements

This book would not be possible if not for the vision God put in my heart to help inspire young people from all over. The last thing I ever thought I would do is write a book, but my thirst is real for helping young people see their dreams realized. There were moments I wanted to quit, but God was my rock.

I was also blessed with wonderful friends and family members, who have given me faith, hope and love to see this project through. There is not enough paper for me to thank everyone individually so I've decided to just list everyone by category below. Without you all this vision would not come to pass. It's your hydrating me that helped me to finish this task. The man that hated reading now writes a book for teenagers all over the world to read. Wow!

Family: My Dad and My Mom, my brothers Mikey and David, My Uncle Joey, My Aunts Leslie, Gerda, Kettly, cousins Rowena and Daphne. God blessed me with an amazing group of family members, and there are many more I've left out here.

Friends: My beautiful girlfriend Marsha who has been my partner in this project from the start.

Cleveland, Arnel, Jesse, Victor, Carl, Gritz, Steven aka Mr. Esteyban, Tina, Peta-Gaye, Lacey, Shanay, Sammetra, Candace, Tamara, Darius, Mackenzie, Lisa Linder, Lenise; you all have blessed me with your prayers, your time brainstorming with me, and your love. I'm sure there are many friends I've failed to mention that are more recent in years like Larry Goodman, Genice Reid, Andres Gonzalez, the list goes on and on.

Mentors: Paul Reddick, Monte Sanders, Laymon Hicks, Ray Lewis #52 (GOAT LB), Ryan Lee; thank you all for your teachings, for the experiences you've shared with me. Also, I must include all my high school football coaches, Coach Bowen, Coach Ruocco, Coach Marinello, Coach Wiggins, Coach Nick, Coach Mann, and Coach Chris.

Spiritual Teachers/Family: Pastor Jim Cymbala, Pastor Todd Crews & Transitions, Pastor Tim Dilena. Great leaders are hard to find, and my spirit is at an all-time high because of you guys.

I'd like to also thank the HOSA students from Maxwell H.S. and my experience at the Yogi Berra Museum. Those opportunities to speak helped fuel me like no other. Thanks to all that made that possible.

Last but not least I'd like to thank you, the reader of this book. I don't know how you got this book, but I prayed that you'd receive it. There's nothing more I wanted then to help you find what you love and for you to do it for the rest of your life. I believe that the contents you learn in this book are the ingredient all successful people have, a blueprint they all live by. You now have that blueprint and I thank you for letting me share it with you.

About the Author

G eo Derice is an inspirational youth speaker who has dedicated his life to helping young people live out their dreams and maximize their full potential. He travels around the U.S. speaking to young people about what it takes to reach the top, how to stand out from the crowd, and how to help others to do the same.

His message of hope is exactly what today's young people need to push through their troubled pasts and shortcomings. Through stories of redemption, which are both funny and heart breaking at times, young people are able to learn how to make the most of their lives.

Most importantly, he is a real down to earth person who simply cares. No one cares what you have to say until you show how much you care. After hearing Geo speak—that's something you'll have no doubt about.

Committed to a life of serving young people, Geo is well on his way to inspire thousands, if not millions, to see their hopes and dreams realized.

Interested in having Geo come speak to your
school, church, or organization?
To Book Geo Derice
Please email info@geospeaks.com
Or visit www.Geospeaks.com

We Need to Hear from You!!!!

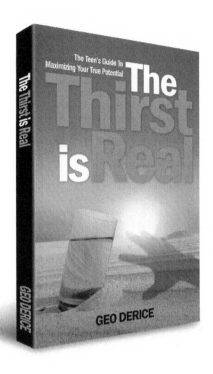

Thank you for completing the book "The Thirst Is Real". We want to give you an opportunity today to become a "water fountain" for someone else. The best way for you to do this is by leaving a review on the book on Amazon.com. You can do so by going to the following link:

http://amzn.to/1lRuXlS

Your review of the book will help someone else who might be on the fence on whether or not this book will help them or not. Without your support this book will not be able to impact those who need it most! Please take 60 seconds to post a review and share your thoughts on the book.

I cannot thank you enough for reading the book and thank you in advance for leaving a review. Your words will help get this book in the hands of many others like you.

Sincerely,

Geo Derice

Geo speaking with the Springfield Gardens High School football team in Queens, NY.

This speech came after a two-game losing streak where the football team lost by a combined total of two points. They would go on to win four out of their next six games, to finish their best season at 5-4 and clinch a playoff birth. The team carried the diagram in the photo to every ball game as added inspiration.

**Geo inspiring a group of young men at
Yogi Berra Museum**

Geo gave an inspirational speech at the Yogi Berra
Museum where he taught the kids to never give up on
their dreams, to treat others the way they'd like to be
treated, and of the value of working hard.
The young men left very inspired and were overjoyed
(as you can see in the photo above).

**Geo meeting with students of HOSA at Maxwell H.S.
in Brooklyn, NY.**

This group featured many bright minds who are all
interested in making an impact in the medical field.

Ian Ladouceur and Geo Derice

Ian was Geo's little brother from the Big Brothers Big Sisters of NYC for 1.5 years. Ian is a bright kid who was often misunderstood by many, but a child with a heart of gold who loves to help others.

**Starting Quarterback of the Sheepshead Bay Sharks
Scottie Denis and Geo.**

Scottie has been a mentee of Geo for several years and this year finally had his dream of playing varsity quarterback realized. This photo was taken after Scottie led his football team to a key victory against Beach Channel H.S. 30-0.

Ray Lewis of the Baltimore Ravens with Geo

Ray Lewis is one of Geo's mentors. Geo's own life has been inspired by Mr. Lewis' dedication to living a life of passion, and to leaving a legacy for others to follow.

**At the private screening for the movie "42"
in Brooklyn, NY.**

Geo spoke to a theater full of young people about the life of Jackie Robinson and the secret to fulfilling your true potential.

Michael Derice(left), Hall of Famer Quarterback Joe Namath (middle), and Geo Derice (right)

Geo and his brother Michael with Joe Namath at the Joe Namath Football Camp at Western Connecticut State University.

Daymond John (left) and Geo Derice (right)

Founder of Fubu, and Shark Tank's own Daymond John and Geo Derice at the DotcomXpo Conference in Stamford, Connecticut.

Download Your Free Copy of The Thirst Is Real Worksheet by visiting:

www.mythirstisreal.com/worksheet

There you will find the top questions to ask yourself from the book and begin your path to chasing and capturing what you've always dreamed.

It's complete free, simply go to the website address above to download it today!

Made in the USA
Middletown, DE
17 January 2019